PERSONAL FINANCE: BASIC TIPS

PERSONAL FINANCE

BASIC TIPS

 PERSONAL FINANCE: BASIC TIPS

 PERSONAL FINANCE: BASIC TIPS

INDEX

Introduction

Make an assessment

Setting goals for successful financial planning

Decide your spending wisely

Dealing with the mountains of debt and credit

Everything you need to know about taxes

Jumping into the right insurance plan

How to get help from professional financial experts

Do-it-yourself with personal finance software

Savings and compound interest

Smart Investment Steps

Conclusion

PERSONAL FINANCE: BASIC TIPS

Introduction

Being on top and aware of one's financial situation will definitely be an advantage that most people should make sure they have. This awareness will give them the opportunity to capitalize on situations should good business arise. Get all the information you need in this book!

<u>Empower your personal finances: Unlocking the major obstacles to personal financial freedom</u>

When you know your financial situation well, there are always areas where this knowledge will help you create better investment opportunities and platforms. This knowledge and regular assessment can also help turn any current financial routine into a booming investment opportunity. With the use of financial information, you can also make decisions that ensure a healthy financial condition.

Make an assessment

This will also ensure help for the person who is trying to curb negative spending habits. When an active assessment is performed periodically, you will eventually be able to identify areas that need attention or control. Sometimes the information learned from the assessment exercise can be really shocking, as it usually sheds light on the situation in a very detailed way.

Most people undertake the assessment exercise to understand their current position and how they can make adjustments to accommodate any investments for the future. If financial security for the future is not taken into account, many problems will occur over time when the person is unable to support themselves and their dependents.

Financial assessments can also help you consider making other, more important lifestyle decisions. These can take the form of investments in property, businesses, retirement plans, and any other type of exercise that is financially beneficial. With better planning made easier, you can then explore other enjoyable avenues such as vacations, hobbies that require substantial financial commitments, and any other commitments that require substantial financial outlay.

 PERSONAL FINANCE: BASIC TIPS

Setting goals for successful financial planning

Ideally, everyone should have some sort of financial planning. The sooner you begin this particular exercise, the better the chances are that you will be in a position to take advantage of the opportunities.

Where to Start

The following are some of the elements to explore in the pursuit of setting goals for successful financial planning:

- Setting measurable financial goals is an exercise that should be done very early on for the individual. With this type of planning firmly in place, the goal can be achieved, as the individual remains focused on the objectives. This also helps to design a plan that involves very detailed goals, in their basic commitments.

- There should also be some measurable financial goals that allow the individual to budget accordingly. Understanding the implications of financial commitments will certainly be a necessary factor when considering investments as a whole. Since each investment affects the other, every detail should be clearly delineated when the goal-setting process is in the planning stage.

- Periodic assessment of the individual's financial and investment situation should be a practice that is incorporated into any goal-setting exercise. Since several changes may have occurred after the previous assessment, it would be prudent for the person to reconsider investments that have not had the desired return, allowing the person to make any necessary adjustments he or she deems appropriate.

- Planning as early in life as possible will allow the individual to explore the possibility of setting various goals, which would eventually help bring the investments to maturity at the convenient time of perhaps retirement. When options are explored with a realistic mindset, the goal-setting exercise will ensure that the individual is better able to deal with possible deviations of any kind.

PERSONAL FINANCE: BASIC TIPS

Decide your spending wisely

When it comes to finances, most people seem to have trouble making decisions about how their money should be spent and how to make wise choices that would affect their financial future. There is a lot of information available, but finding ways to put this information to work for yourself is the trick to getting your finances in order.

What's going on

The following are some tips on how to decide on a spending habit that would be wise and

prudent:

- Perhaps one of the best tips you can give would be to learn to use cash as much as possible, rather than resort to seemingly convenient credit cards. Any other form of transaction that does not involve cash has a tendency to cause the individual to spend without having a clear and controlled amount in mind, therefore, the individual is often unaware of his spending habits until he is confronted with the credit card or other financial statements.

- Deferring the purchase of items that would involve large amounts of money unless most or all of the payment can be made in cash is another prudent way to handle finances. This will help the person focus

better on saving for the item and also avoid having to pay phenomenal interest rates when payments are made on a loan plan.

- Learning to negotiate the best deal when shopping is a good way to spend wisely and still get the best deal. It will also help the individual gain skills that could help him or her in other areas of life. It also helps to learn to develop the habit of being strong and walking away if the price doesn't fit the budget.

- Designing an appropriate budget and sticking strictly to it will help the individual adhere to prudent spending habits. This is because everything has been carefully planned and clearly laid out, thus giving the individual a sense of each expense incurred.

 PERSONAL FINANCE: BASIC TIPS

Dealing with the mountains of debt and credit

When struggling to deal with a mountain of debt that doesn't seem to be going away, no matter how much effort you put into stopping the spending habit, it's usually a very stressful and complicated affair.

However, all is not lost, as there are some exercises that can be used to bring some calm to the debt and credit situation.

PERSONAL FINANCE: BASIC TIPS

Take a good look

The following are some of the areas that should be considered when examining debt management and credit lines:

- One of the first steps to take is to face the financial situation head on and take the time to understand the situation in detail. By doing so, the individual is able to make important decisions and is definitely more aware of how to best manage debt by considering some viable ways to reduce it.

- Writing down all the financial figures in and out will help the individual make some adjustments and make an informed decision about which debts should be encumbered and prioritized over others.

This should be decided on the basis of the interest earned on the debts, thus helping in some way not to accumulate more debt.

- Contacting creditors with the intention of redesigning the debt situation to make it more manageable will also be an option to consider. Most debtors are willing to help, as it would eventually mean that they too would benefit from having the debt paid in full. Simply continuing with the current payment terms will not help and may even cause more problems when the initial amount is not repaid and the payments only serve to cover the interest incurred.

- While this may incur some cost, seeking the help of a professional financial planner should also be explored as an option for finding ways to manage the mountain of debt. These professionals will be able to provide a better view of how to handle the issues in the best interest of the individual.

PERSONAL FINANCE: BASIC TIPS

Everything you need to know about taxes

Most people mistakenly assume that taxes are intended to be paid simply without default and according to the terms of the forms or invoices submitted. Few take the time to understand the system that calculates taxes, so it does not give them the space to make the claims that would help minimize the amounts taxed.

Reduce Taxes

If a concerted effort is made to understand the tax systems, the individual may also find opportunities to apply for and obtain privileges. These privileges are good because they ideally put the money back into the individual's hand and allow more possibilities for savings, where the money can be used for other legitimate purposes.

The following are some areas that can be explored with the specific intent of trying to reduce taxes through privilege:

- Deductions can be made by reducing the amounts of income on which the person is taxed. Calculations are made on gross income and these deductions are applied if the gross income falls below a certain amount. There are also deductions that can be calculated when there are spouses and dependent children in the equation. These incurred expenses can be used as an item

that would facilitate adjustments to total income, thus providing a good platform to capitalize on for deductions.

- There are also possibilities in certain circumstances where medical bills can be used as possible tax exemption tools. This is especially the dependent party, which incurs such a bill in the long run and there is no outside help from the governing body. Applications for these financial commitments to be included in the list of tax exemptions.

- Personal expenses can also be used to claim tax deductions, especially if some of these expenses come in the form of support for other worthy causes and charities.

Jumping into the right insurance plan

When it comes to choosing the right insurance coverage, the individual is often influenced by the sales pitch given by the agent trying to sell the policy. There is a great deal of trust, as the individual depends heavily on the advice of the agent selling the plan.

Most people do not take the time to read every detail of the policy they want before making a long-term financial commitment to the insurance plan. This, of course, is quite foolish, but often the most common scenario when it comes to buying an insurance plan.

Which plan to choose?

The following are some types of insurance plans that are supposed to be more useful to the individual and are an appropriate long-term investment to consider:

- Indemnity Plans: This usually comes in the form of a pre-set deductible figure and offers the highest degree of flexibility with respect to the care expected and received.

- Preferred Provider Organization Plan: this insurance plan provides the individual with relevant health coverage that is mostly from a designated set of facilities and panels. If the individual chooses to use his or her own medical expertise, the premium will be charged accordingly and will generally be higher.

- Healthcare organization and maintenance plans: In this case there is an option to choose the primary care physician from a pre-determined list of healthcare providers. Claims can then be made on the policy if the services of such a facility are requested at any given time. This type of coverage is usually quite general and may not really cover more severe or specialized needs.

- There are also life insurance plans and educational plans that may be considered for obvious reasons.

How to get help from professional financial experts

Most people work hard to be able to enjoy the finer things in life, or at least to be able to live a fairly comfortable existence. There are many financial commitments that would require an individual's attention, and these commitments grow faster and faster as one venture into more spending needs.

Professional Help

Getting the help of a financial planner is sometimes not only wise, but may be necessary to ensure that the individual does not become over-committed financially. Some of the decisions made could make the individual's situation useless and crippling in the long run.

The following are some of the areas where a financial expert will be able to provide appropriate advice so that the individual has the information necessary to facilitate an informed choice about a financial commitment scheme:

- A financial professional will be able to advice on planned investments, as their knowledge in these areas will be more in-depth and detailed. Proper guidance will help the individual make a better and more informed choice of appropriate investments. These professionals are able to calculate risks and show figures that would balance the investment well to show benefits or show a possible loss if the investment is not prudent to commit to.

- Financial experts can also provide guidance and information for retirement plans and other financial commitments, which would allow the individual to enjoy the same or similar quality of life during the retirement phase. Assistance provided in this area will enable the individual to make good decisions based on the information learned.

 PERSONAL FINANCE: BASIC TIPS

Do-it-yourself with personal finance software

For those who are internet savvy, there are also many other options available where the individual will be able to get the software that allows the financial planning exercise to be explored. This is ideal for those who really don't have time to meet with a personal financial planner or who don't want to be bothered by unwanted solicitations.

Software Help

This financial planning software can result in different investments and advice, depending on the information provided by the client, who in this case is the person seeking such assistance. The investment plans offered are usually in line with the information provided by the individual and are therefore more suitable, as all possible plans are explored before the appropriate plan is tailored to the individual's financial capabilities.

Detailed instructions for all financial software will allow almost anyone with a basic knowledge of Microsoft Excel to use the material provided in the best way possible without having to incur the high costs that come with using a financial planner. Many comparisons can be facilitated through the financial software by simply typing in the different scenarios and this can be done infinitely. There is no possibility of exhausting the limits of the software by feeding it variable financial information often, however, this is not possible with a financial planner, as the person would soon become irritated and exhausted with all the different styles the client wants to try.

One of the most popular software that is often used is the fully integrated financial planning software suite that provides all of the following: retirement software options, budget and cash flow projections, net worth projections, multiple college student projections.

Comprehensive asset allocation planning and projections. These softwares are linked together for complete integration and are sometimes able to provide more competitive assistance than the financial planner.

 PERSONAL FINANCE: BASIC TIPS

Savings and compound interest

Being able to get the maximum benefit from an amount of savings is something most people would like to be able to enjoy, but this is not always possible, as not many people are aware of the benefits of choosing an appropriate savings plan that offers such "rewards".

Which plan is right for you?

When it comes to the savings plan that allows interest to accumulate and then compound, it is worth the effort and time it takes to explore this in depth. In very basic terms, this would really mean that the interest earned from the savings plan will allow the individual to enjoy an additional amount of interest over and above the existing interest. Although it may seem very theoretical, it is possible to find savings and compound interest plans that suit the financial commitment needs of almost all investors.

The basic concept applied to this type of plan would ideally be to set aside a fixed sum, however small it may seem, to be deposited in a savings plan that supplies the compound interest platform. When this commitment is seriously put into practice without any possibility of hesitation, the accumulated amounts can be quite amazing and this will help motivate the person to stay in it longer and more diligently. The main idea behind this style of saving would be to keep the

money in the savings plans as long as possible and ensure that the billing is done in a firm and committed way.

Interest rates for these plans are generally calculated on a daily basis, which will present an overall better option for the person interested in capitalizing on the small amounts invested.

 PERSONAL FINANCE: BASIC TIPS

Smart Investment Steps

It is possible to make smart investment plans without too many complications and detailed paperwork. The key to smart investment plans lies primarily in the ability to understand and make smart decisions. Taking the time and effort to thoroughly understand the investment plan before committing to it would be the best way to realize the idea of smart investing.

A few tips

The following are some points to consider in the quest to ensure that investments made are beneficial to the individual both in their

current form and in the long-term scenario:

- Ensuring that the effort to understand the particular requirements and benefits dictated by the chosen plan is perhaps the most important exploration exercise to be embarked upon. Without this knowledge, the individual would be basing his or her commitment on the rumors of others and this can be crazy when the payments do not match the perceived promise of the plan.

- Do not be lulled into a financial commitment until all aspects of the plan have been fully understood. Many people are so overwhelmed by the sales pitch presented that they don't take the time to really read the fine print of the plan being presented.

PERSONAL FINANCE: BASIC TIPS

- They are always wary of plans that advertise "free" benefits, as these are often linked to other commitments that are not normally explained and may never really be explored until the opportunity arises, when the "free" elements are invoked by the investor. In most cases it is only then that the investor discovers that the "free" addition is not really as first perceived.

- Remember that you should only commit to what can be paid for at that time. Overextending yourself is not a good idea, as it could cause the individual to default on the investment and lose everything he or she has already committed to.

Conclusion

Keeping good control of your financial affairs can sometimes be a very difficult task. Using the above tips should become a walk in the park. Start living a much more comfortable life, stop worrying about finances and enjoy your life!

Visit our author page on Amazon and get more MENTES LIBRES!

http://amazon.com/author/menteslibres

If you wish, you can leave a comment on this book by clicking on the following link so that we can continue to grow! Thank you very much for your purchase!

https://www.amazon.com/dp/B086KV86TM

www.ingramcontent.com/pod-product-compliance
Lightning Source LLC
Chambersburg PA
CBHW050305220526
45465CB00002B/839